Wild Cats

Written by Janine Amos
Reading consultants: Christopher Collier and Alan Howe,
Bath Spa University, UK

This edition published by Parragon in 2009
Parragon
Queen Street House
4 Queen Street
Bath BA1 1HE, UK

ISBN 978-1-4075-3797-9
Printed in China

Wild Cats

LIVE. LEARN. DISCOVER.

Bath New York Singapore Hong Kong Cologne Delhi Melbourne

Parents' notes

This book is part of a series of non-fiction books designed to appeal to children learning to read.

Each book has been developed with the help of educational experts.

At the end of each book is a quiz to help your child remember the information and the meanings of some of the words and sentences. There is also a glossary of difficult words relating to the subject matter in the book, and an index.

Contents

6   What is a wild cat?

8   Types of wild cat

10 Wild world

12 Family life

14 Lion

16 Hunting

18 Tiger

20 Keep off!

22 Leopard

24 Taking care of wild cats

26 Quiz

28 Glossary

30 Index

What is a wild cat?

A wild cat is a mammal with a coat of fur. Wild cats live in most parts of the world. Wild cats eat meat and are smart hunters.

The **lion** is one of the biggest wild cats. Only male lions have manes.

mane

paw

claws

A tiger is the largest wild cat. Siberian tigers are the biggest cats of all.

The **Scottish wild cat** is about the size of a pet cat.

A **cheetah** is the fastest wild cat—and one of the world's fastest animals.

coat

tail

Types of wild cat

There are lots of different kinds, or species, of wild cat. Some are a solid color. Some are spotted or striped.

Tiger
The tiger is a big cat. It is orange with thick, black stripes.

Ocelot
The medium-sized ocelot has both spots and stripes.

Over short distances, the cheetah can run as fast as a car!

Mountain lion (puma)

The mountain lion, or puma, has a solid gray or brown coat.

Lynx

The lynx is medium-sized. It has a short tail and furry ears.

Leopard

The leopard is a big cat with spots called rosettes.

9

Wild world

Wild cats live in many parts of the world— in hot deserts, cold mountains, and thick forests. Each species of cat is suited to the place in which it lives.

Forests—jaguar
Jaguars live in forests. They are good tree climbers. Their long tails help them balance.

Forest jaguars have dark fur for hiding in the shadows.

Mountains— snow leopard

The snow leopard can live in high, cold places. It has thick fur to keep warm.

Deserts—bobcat

The bobcat has furry feet to protect it from the hot ground.

Family life

The babies of most kinds of wild cat are called cubs. The mother protects them and keeps them warm.

Mothers move their cubs out of danger. They carry them gently in their mouths.

Lion cubs are covered in spots! Their spotted fur helps hide them from enemies.

Mother cats clean their cubs by licking them.

At first the cubs feed on milk from their mother.

Cubs play-fight to practice hunting skills.

Lion

Lions live in family groups called prides. Father lions protect the pride, warning off strangers with loud roars. Lionesses (female lions) do most of the hunting.

Lions live together as one big family. The biggest prides live in grasslands, where they hunt large animals such as zebras.

DiscoveryFact™

Lions spend about 20 hours a day resting—or taking a catnap!

A father and mother lion look different from each other. The father has a shaggy mane around his head.

This picture shows a pride of lions drinking at a water hole.

Hunting

Wild cats are made for hunting. They have good senses. They can see, hear, and smell their prey from far away.

Cats move quickly and silently when they hunt.

Their weapons are their strong jaws and long, curved claws.

male lion   tiger   Scottish wildcat   cheetah

stripes   mountain lion   lynx   ocelot   leopard

forest jaguar   snow leopard   bobcat   jaguar

cub   mother   lioness   pride   serval   tail

spots   buffalo   ear   desert   mountain   forest

paw print   grass   leaf   Iberian lynx

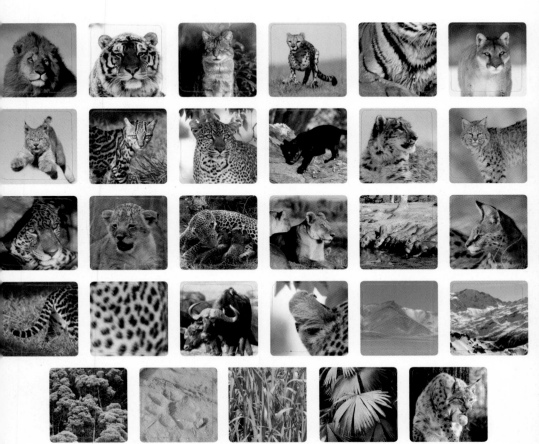

The serval has such good hearing it can hear small animals moving underground!

Mother cats take their cubs on hunting trips. The cubs learn by watching and copying their mother.

Wild cats have powerful back legs for chasing their prey.

Tigers and other cats leap and pounce when they hunt.

Tiger

Tigers are big and powerful cats—but they are hard to see in their wild homes. Their striped coats blend in with the grass and leaves.

Tigers are good swimmers. On hot days they keep cool in water.

DiscoveryFact™

Fewer than 1,000 Siberian tigers live in the wild today. People have killed many of them.

Tigers can climb trees to keep watch for their prey. When hunting, they watch their prey from the shadows, then rush out and attack.

Tigers feed on large animals, such as deer and buffalo.

Keep off!

Cats move across the same area of land every day. This area is called a territory.

Big cats roar to warn others to keep off their territory.

Experts track wild cats by following paw prints in the earth.

Cats rub their furry bodies against trees. The scent from their fur stays on the tree.

Cats mark out their territory. They leave behind their smell, or scent, by spraying.

Leopard

Leopards are strong cats and good climbers. They spend a lot of time hiding in trees, resting, and watching for prey.

Sometimes leopards attack from above, then drag their prey into the branches for a treetop meal.

Leopards rest in trees. Their spotted coats help them hide in the leaves.

Leopards hunt alone and at night. They live in forests, on grasslands, and in the mountains.

Leopard cubs shelter in dens in hollow trees, rocks, or caves. Their mother looks after them.

Taking care of wild cats

The world's wild cats are in danger. People have hunted them for their fur or destroyed their habitats (the places where they live).

Some wild cats live in reserves, where they are kept safe from hunters.

DiscoveryFact™

Tourists can visit some reserves. It is an amazing way of seeing wildlife up close.

People have trapped and killed snow leopards for their fur. Today there are laws to protect them.

There are only 100 Iberian lynxes left in the wild. Their habitat is now protected land.

Quiz

Now try this quiz! All the answers can be found in this book.

What do wild cats eat?

(a) Meat
(b) Biscuits
(c) Plants

Which is the fastest wild cat?

(a) The lion
(b) The tiger
(c) The cheetah

Where do jaguars live?

(a) Forests
(b) Deserts
(c) Mountains

What is the name of a family of lions?

(a) A pack
(b) A pride
(c) A school

How many Siberian tigers live in the wild today?

(a) Over 1 million
(b) Over 10,000
(c) Under 1,000

Where do leopards like to rest?

(a) In a bed
(b) On the ground
(c) In a tree

Glossary

Coat   The fur of a wild cat.

Cub   A baby wild cat.

Den   A wild cat's home, such as a cave or a hollow tree.

Lioness   A female lion.

Mammal   An animal with hair or fur, which feeds its babies on milk.

Mane   Thick fur around the neck of a lion.

Prey   The animal that a wild
           cat hunts for food.

Pride   A group of lions that
           live together.

Reserve   Land where wild cats
           can live in safety.

Senses   To see, hear, taste,
           touch, and smell.

Species   Animals of the same kind.
           All lions belong to one species,
           all tigers belong to another.

Index

b

biggest wild cat 7
bobcats 11
buffalo 19

c

cheetahs 7, 9
claws 16
coats 6, 7, 9, 18, 23
colors 8, 9
cubs 12-13, 17, 23

d

deer 19
dens 23
deserts 11

e

ears 9, 17

f

families 12-15
fastest wild cat 7, 9
fathers 14, 15
forests 10, 11, 23
fur 6, 11, 21, 25

g

grasslands 14, 23

h

habitat destruction 24
hunting 6, 13, 14, 16-17,
    19, 23, 24

i

Iberian lynxes 25

j

jaguars 10, 11
jaws 16

l

leopards 9, 22-23
lionesses 14
lions 6, 13, 14-15
lynxes 9, 25

m

mammals 6
manes 6, 15
meat eaters 6
milk 13
mothers 12, 13, 15, 17,
    23
mountain lions (pumas) 9
mountains 11, 23

o

ocelots 8

p

paw prints 21
play-fight 13
prey 16, 17, 19, 22, 23
prides 14, 15

r

reserves 24
resting 14, 22, 23
roaring 14, 20

s

scent 21
Scottish wild cats 7
senses 16
servals 17
Siberian tigers 7, 18
snow leopards 11, 25
species 8
spots 8, 9, 13, 23
spraying 21
stripes 8, 18
swimming 18

t

tails 7, 9, 10
territory 20, 21
tigers 7, 8, 17, 18-19
tourists 24
tracking wild cats 21
trapping and killing wild

cats 18, 24, 25
tree climbing 10, 19, 22

w

water holes 15

z

zebras 14, 17

Acknowledgments

t=top, c=center, b=bottom, r=right, l=left

Cover: Jeff Vanuga/CORBIS

p.3 Jeff Vanuga/Corbis, p.4t Joe McDonald/Corbis, p.5 Tom Brakefield/Corbis, p.5tl Joe McDonald/Corbis, p.5bl DLILLC/Corbis, p.6-7 Joe McDonald/Corbis, p.7tl Kevin Schafer/Corbis, p.7tr Steve Austin; Papilio/Corbis, p.7br Renee Lynn/Corbis, p.8-9 Randy Wells/Corbis, p.8br Darrell Gulin/Corbis, p.9tl DLILLC/Corbis, p.9tr Joe McDonald/Corbis, p.9bl Alan & Sandy Carey/zefa/Corbis, p.9br Joe McDonald/Corbis, p.10-11 Frans Lemmens/zefa/Corbis, p.11tl Jim Zuckerman/Corbis, p.11tr Alan & Sandy Carey/zefa/Corbis, p.11br DLILLC/Corbis, p.12-13 Joe McDonald/Corbis, p.13tl Gabriela Staebler/zefa/Corbis, p.13tr Michael Kooren/Reuters/Corbis, p.13m Tom Brakefield/Corbis, p.13br Renee Lynn/Corbis, p.14-15 Paul A. Souders/Corbis, p.14br Stephen Frink/Corbis, p.15tl Randy Wells/Corbis, p.15tr Gallo Images/Corbis, p.16 DLILLC/Corbis, p.17tr DLILLC/Corbis, p.17ml Terry W. Eggers/Corbis, p.17bl Tom Brakefield/zefa/Corbis, p.17br Jeff Vanuga/Corbis, p.18-19 Tom Brakefield/Corbis, p.19tr DLILLC/Corbis, p.19br Ronnie Kaufman/Corbis, p.20 Renee Lynn/Corbis, p.21t Martin Harvey/Corbis, p.21bl Konrad Wothe/Getty, p.21br Theo Allofs/Corbis, p.22-23 Gallo Images/Corbis, p.23tr Joseph Van Os/Getty, p.23m John Conrad/Corbis, p.23bl Gallo Images/Corbis, p.24-25 Gabriela Staebler/zefa/Corbis, p.24bl Ikachan /Dreamstime.com, p.25tr DLILLC/Corbis, p.25br Jazzer/Dreamstime.com, p.27b Joe McDonald/Corbis

Additional images used on sticker sheet: bottom row, first sticker: Dennis Sabo/Dreamstime.com